IN THE VALLEY OF ALLAH

An INFIDEL's View of Islam, The Islamic State

and Terrorism

By: Darren W. Freeman

Disclaimer

ROYAL CREEK PUBLISHING HOUSE 2022

Table of Contents;

Chapter One

Islamic fundamentalism has been defined as a puritanical, revivalist, and reform movement of Muslims who aim to return to the founding scriptures of Islam. Islamic fundamentalists are of the view that Muslim-majority countries should return to the fundamentals of an Islamic state that truly shows the essence of the system of Islam, in terms of its socio-politico-economic system. Islamic fundamentalists favor "a literal and originalist interpretation" of the primary sources of Islam (the Quran, Hadith, and Sunnah), seek to eliminate (what they perceive to be) "corrupting" non-Islamic influences from every part of their lives, and see "Islamic fundamentalism" as a pejorative term used by outsiders for Islamic revivalism and Islamic activism.

Definitions do vary as to what 'Islamic fundamentalism" exactly is and how, if at all, it differs from Islamism (or political Islam) or Islamic revivalism. The term fundamentalism has been deemed "misleading" by those who suggest that all mainstream Muslims believe in

4

the literal divine origin and perfection of the Quran and are therefore "fundamentalists", and others who believe it is a term that is used by outsiders in order to describe perceived trends within Islam. Professor of religious studies at Georgetown University, John L. Esposito have criticised the term "Islamic Fundamentalism" due to its ambigous nature; as well as due to its usage being heavily influenced through a Western lens of American Protestantism and Christian presuppositions. According to him, the more appropriate terms would be "Islamic revivalism" and "Islamic activism", since the traditions of Tajdid (revival) *and Islah* (reform) are rooted within the Islamic religious history, from the early Islamic centuries to the contemporary times. During the 1990s, the post-Soviet states borrowed the Western Rhetoric of "Islamic fundamentalism" and used it as a synonym for "Wahhabism"(Movement, Musli Brotherhood & Jihad), another label.

Some Islamic fundamentalists include Sayyid Qutb, Ibn Saud, Abul Ala Mawdudi, and Israr Ahmed. The Wahhabi movement and its funding by Saudi Arabia is often described as being responsible for the popularity of contemporary Islamic fundamentalism. From this specific regional context, islamic fundamentalism can be seen as a branch of the West.

The modern Islamic fundamentalist movements have their origins in the late 19th century. The Syrian-Egyptian Salafi scholar Rashid Rida (1865-1935 C.E) was the first major theologian to comprehensively elucidate the foundational principles of an Islamic state in its modern iteration, and these doctrines would be readily adopted by later Islamic fundamentalists. According to the Arab poet Adunis, the Islamic World experienced an influx of European ideas, values and thoughts during the late nineteenth-century. The thinkers in the Muslim world reacted to modernity in three major ways.

Secularists like Mirza Aqa Khan Kermani, Mustafa Kemal Ataturk, etc considered Islam to be responsible for the backwardness of Muslims; gradually abandoning religion and adopting Western ideas. Meanwhile, Modernists like Muhammad Abduh in Egypt advocated reforms to reconcile with modernity; while emphasizing adherence to basic Islamic ideals. A third current; widely known as Islamic fundamentalism, pioneered by Rashid

Rida across the Arab world and Abul A'ala Mawdudi (1903-1979 C.E) in South Asia, asserted that Islam is relevant for all times and must reign supreme. They idealised the era of Prophet Muhammad and his companions, and sought to revive its "purity" and early Islamic power. For them, the economic, political and military problems of the Islamic World are due to Muslim negligence in strictly adhering to the tenets of SHARIA.

In reviewing the Wahhabi movement, an Arabian fundamentalist movement that began in the 18th century, gained traction and spread during the 19th and 20th centuries. After the First World War, Rashid Rida would be highly influenced by the Hanbali puritanical and revivalist doctrines of the 13th century Hanbalite theologian Ibn Taymiyya and the Wahabbi movement. He began to ardently campaign against Western influence and modernist ideas. The ideas of Rashid Rida, who is widely regarded as the spiritual father of the Salafiyya movement, marks the rise of Islamic fundamentalist movements. He advocated fundamentalist causes through the early Islamic journal *Al-Manar* that operated for about thirty-five years and popularized his political theory of Islamic state after

7

the First World War; as an alternative model against rising currents of secularism and nationalism.

During the Cold War following World War II, some NATO governments, particularly those of the United States and the United Kingdom, launched covert and overt campaigns to encourage and strengthen fundamentalist groups in the Middle East and southern Asia. These groups were seen as a hedge against potential expansion by the Soviet Union, and as a means to prevent the growth of nationalistic movements that were not necessarily favorable toward the interests of the Western nations. By the 1970s, the Islamists had become important allies in supporting governments, such as Egypt, which were friendly to U.S. interests. By the late 1970s, however, some fundamentalist groups had become militaristic leading to threats and changes to existing regimes. The overthrow of the Shah in Iran and rise of the Ayatollah Khomeini was one of the most significant signs of this shift. Subsequently, fundamentalist forces in Algeria caused a civil war, caused a near-civil war in Egypt, and caused the downfall of the Soviet occupation in Afghanistan.

Muslim critics of Islamic fundamentalism often draw a parallel between the modern fundamentalist movement and the 7th century Khawarij sect. From their essentially political position, the Kharijites developed extreme doctrines that set them apart from both mainstream Sunni and Shia Muslims. The Kharijites were particularly noted for adopting a radical approach to Takfir (is a controversial concept in Islamist discourse, denoting excommunication, as one Muslim declaring another Muslim as a non-believer (kafir)., whereby they declared other Muslims to be unbelievers and therefore deemed them worthy of death.

Chapter Two

The SECULAR STATE

Islamic fundamentalism's push for *sharia* and an Islamic

state has come into conflict with conceptions of

the secular, democratic state, such as the internationally

supported Universal Declaration of Human Rights.

Anthony J. Dennis notes that "Western and Islamic visions

of the state, the individual and society are not only

divergent, they are often totally at odds." Among human

rights disputed by fundamentalist Muslims are:

- Freedom from religious police
- Equality issues between men and women
- Separation of religion and state
- Freedom of speech
- Freedom of religion

In reviewing this one, it sees that words do not always reflect actions. In the SECULAR world all religions would be free to practice their faith free from persecution and a Deocratic ideological society would emerge. BUT, this is in direct opposite actions taken upon by the Islamic set that fosters Non-diversity, exclusion and condemnation of other beliefs and faiths.

An example is the "Medina State" established in western Arabia by the Prophet in 622 CE is commonly cited in Islamic discourse as the model of an Islamic state that will enforce Sharia. That model is projected in modern constitutional terms as a fully developed state ruled by the Prophet as the original and exclusive human sovereign and sole source of law and political authority. That state is believed to have been populated by ideal Muslims, both individually and collectively as a community of devout believers. According to modern Islamists, since they are instructed by the Quran to strictly adhere to the example of the Prophet, Muslims today are religiously obliged to seek to re-enact the model of the Medina state in their respective post-colonial nation-states.

"This is where conflict begins"...(Darren W Freeman).

The incompatibility of SHARIA, and CONSTITUTIONAL RIGHTS/ The thought there should be a separation of Church and State are and have been a Western Civiliation Model, that is rejected by SHARIA, that shows no difference between Church and State and that one thought or one religious belief must be accepted by all without question. To be a Muslim and reject SHARIA has caused the deaths of many.

The thought of Islamists' anachronistic projection of the modern state and its constitutional order into the ancient past is accepted for the sake of argument. It is clear that the model of the "Medina State" cannot be replicated today because the role of the Prophet in their view was unique and cannot be repeated. Muslims today do not, and cannot, accept the possibility of another Prophet after Muhammad who can govern, or enact Sharia law and enforce it as "divinely ordained". To Muslims of the Medina State, what the Prophet said and did was Islam itself, and for all subsequent generations of Muslims governments can at best seek to implement what fallible human beings can

12

do. Yet the cultural and psychological risk of adherence to the Medina State model remains among Muslims today who support an "unconstitutional model" in which the rulers enjoy unfettered legislative, executive, and judicial powers. This belief contradicts the idea of formal or institutional limitation or separation of powers of rulers.

Muslims have experienced a variety of methods for identifying rulers throughout history, but regardless of the method of selection or appointment, the "Caliph", (the title given to the successor of Mohammed as head of the Moslem state and defender of the faith), enjoyed absolute powers for life because once an oath of allegiance was given, there was no organised and peaceful mechanism for withdrawing or restricting it. As the nature of the state was transformed by European colonialism, Islamists today tend to place modern constitutional and legal constraints on the powers of the state through an expansive re-interpretation of traditional notions of consultation *(shura)* in order to support constitutional and democratic principles in the modern sense. Such efforts may be politically attractive at the time they are invoked, but they can easily be reversed in practice because they lack methodological support in traditional Islamic jurisprudence *(usul al-Fiqh).* Being consistent with the values and institutions of their time, the founding jurists of Sharia did not address the need to limit the powers of the Caliph through notions of the separation of powers or an independent judiciary.

Advocates of the *Sharia,* as an Islamic basis for constitutional democratic governance should first revise the methodology of Islamic jurisprudence to support systematic and coherent reform, instead of opportunistic and arbitrarily selective apologia for political expediency.

In general the enforcement of Sharia through the coercive power or authority of the state repudiates the religious quality of compliance, which must be voluntary and deliberate to be valid. Moreover, the claim that Iran and Saudi Arabia are Islamic states is believed by the fact that each of those two states regards the other as a heresy. So which is "Islamic" and how do we know that? If we take each claim at face value, we would be deadlock on the issue. The fact that it is simply not possible to decide whether either of them is "truly" Islamic, or which has the better claim, shows the inherently political nature of the claim. Yet, the separation of Islam and the state does not mean that Islam and *politics* should or can be separated. This must be distinguish and defined between the state and politics in order to facilitate the regulation of the relationship of Islam and the state through politics, but subject to constitutional safeguards.

The claim to implement the totality of the precepts of Sharia in the everyday life of a society is a contradiction in terms because enforcement through the will of the state is the negation of the religious rationale of the binding force of Sharia. Legal prohibition may increase apparent conformity with religious norms, but that does not justify either enhancing piety by force or the violation of the freedom of religion and other human rights of believers and non-believers alike. Since enforcement by the state requires formal enactment as the law of the land, the legislature of the day will have to choose among equally authoritative but different interpretations of the Quran, (Quran is the holy book of Muslims that was revealed by the prophet Muhammad peace be upon him (PBUH), Full Islamic education is found in the Quran). and Sunna, the body of traditional social and legal custom and practice of the Islamic community. Along with

15

the Qur'ān (the holy book of Islam) and Hadith (recorded sayings of the Prophet Muhammad), it is a major source of Shariah, or Islamic law.. The practical impossibility of enforcing Sharia as positive law is reflected in the fact that such centralized coercive enforcement of Sharia as a code of state law was never attempted in Islamic history until the twentieth century.

Chapter Three

Human Rights Controversy

Some states and movements that are perceived or claimed to be Islamic fundamentalists have been criticized for their human rights record by international organizations. The acceptance of international law on human rights has been somewhat limited even in Muslim countries that are not seen as fundamentalist. Ann Elizabeth Mayer writes that states with a predominantly Muslim population, even when they adopt laws along European lines, are influenced by Islamic rules and precepts of *sharia*, which cause conflict with international law on human rights. According to Mayer, features found in conflict include severe deficiencies in criminal procedure, harsh criminal penalties causing great suffering, discrimination against women and non-Muslims, and prohibition against abandoning the Islamic religion. In 1990, under Saudi leadership, the Organization of Islamic

Cooperation, a group representing all Muslim majority nations, adopted the Cairo Declaration on Human Rights in Islam, which substantially diverges from the 1948 Universal Declaration of Human Rights (UDHR). The Cairo declaration lacks provisions for democratic principles, protection for religious freedom, freedom of association and freedom of the press, as well as equality in rights and equal protection under the law. Further it stipulates that "all the rights and freedoms stipulated in this Declaration are subject to the Islamic *Sharia*.

The Cairo declaration followed years of limited acceptance of the Universal declaration by predominantly Muslim states. As an example, in 1984, Iran's UN representative, Said Raja'i Khorasani, said the following amid allegations of human rights violations, "IRAN", recognized no authority, apart from Islamic law and Conventions, declarations and resolutions or decisions of international organizations, which were contrary to Islam, had no validity in the Islamic Republic of Iran. The Universal Declaration of Human Rights, which represented secular understanding of the Judaeo-Christian tradition, could not be implemented by Muslims and did not accord with the system of values recognized by the Islamic Republic of Iran; this country would therefore not hesitate to violate its provisions." These departures, both theoretical and practical, have resulted in a multitude of practices and cases criticized by international human rights groups. The human rights in Iran, human rights in Saudi Arabia, and those under Taliban rule shows the different treatment of women.

Islamic law prohibits forced conversion, following the Quranic principle that there is "no compulsion in religion" (Quran 2:256). However, episodes of forced conversions have occurred in the history of Islam. Historians believe that forced conversion was rare in Islamic history, and most conversions to Islam were voluntary. Muslim rulers were often more interested in conquest than conversion. Ira Lapidus points towards "interwoven terms of political and economic benefits and of a sophisticated culture and religion" as appealing to the masses. He writes that:

The question of why people convert to Islam has always generated the intense feeling. Earlier generations of European scholars believed that conversions to Islam were made at the point of the sword, and that conquered peoples were given the choice of conversion or death. It is now apparent that conversion by force, while not unknown in Muslim countries, was, in fact, rare. Muslim conquerors ordinarily wished to dominate rather than convert, and most conversions to Islam were voluntary. In most cases, worldly and spiritual motives for conversion blended together. Moreover, conversion to Islam did not necessarily imply a complete turning from an old to a totally new life. While it entailed the acceptance of new religious beliefs and membership in a new religious community, most converts retained a deep attachment to the cultures and communities from which they came.

Muslim scholars like Abu Hanifa and Abu Yusuf stated that the jizya tax should be paid by Non-Muslims (Kuffar) regardless of their religion, some later and also earlier Muslim jurists did not permit Non-Muslims who are not People of the Book or Ahle Kitab (Jews, Christians, Sabians) pay the " jizya" (Poll tax that early Islamic rulers demanded from their non-Muslim subjects). Instead, they only allowed them (non Ahle Kitab) to avoid death by choosing to convert to Islam. Of the four schools of Islamic jurisprudence, the Hanafi and Maliki schools allow polytheists to be granted "dhimmi, (A dhimmi refers to a non-Muslim subject of the Ottoman Empire. Derived from Islamic legal conceptions of membership to society, non-Muslims 'dhimmis' were afforded protection by the state and did not serve in the military, in return for specific taxes) "status, except Arab polytheists. However, the Shafii, Hanbali and Zahiri schools only consider Christians, Jews, and Sabians to be eligible to belong to the dhimmi category.

Wael Hallaq states, that in theory, Islamic religious tolerance only applied to those religious groups that Islamic jurisprudence considered to be monotheistic "People of the Book", i.e. Christians, Jews, and Sabians if they paid the "jizya" tax. Those excluded from the "People of the Book" were only offered two choices: convert to Islam or fight to the death. In practice, the "People of the Book" designation and *dhimmi* status were even extended to the non-monotheistic religions of the conquered peoples, such as Hindus, Jains, Buddhists, and other non-monotheists.

The Druze (A small Middle Eastern religious sect characterized by an eclectic system of doctrines and by a cohesion and loyalty among its core members, they live mostly in Lebanon, Syria, and Israel, with smaller communities in other countries), have frequently experienced persecution by different Muslim regimes such as the Shia Ismaili Fatimid tate, Mamluk, Sunni Ottoman Empire, and Egypt Eyalet. The persecution of the Druze included massacres, demolishing Druze prayer houses and holy places and forced conversion to Islam, but those were no ordinary killings in the Druze's narrative were meant to eradicate the whole community.

In recent times, forced conversions to Islam have been threatened or carried out in the context of war, insurgency and intercommunal violence. Cases affecting thousands of people are reported to have occurred during the Partition of India, the Bangladesh Liberation War, in Pakistan, and areas that had been controlled by ISIS (an Islamic State of Iraq and Syria), also known as ISIL (Islamic State of Iraq and the Levant), is a Sunni Jihadist group with a particularly violent ideology that calls itself a Caliphate and claims religious authority over all Muslims.

Disputed allegations of forced conversion of young women have generated public controversy in Egypt and the United Kingdom.

Chapter Four

Islamic Terrorism

Islamic terrorism (also **Islamist terrorism** or **radical Islamic terrorism**) refers to terrorist acts which are committed by militant Islamists and Islamic extremists which have a religious motivation.

Incidents and fatalities from Islamic terrorism have been concentrated in six Muslim-majority countries (Iraq, Afghanistan, Nigeria, Pakistan, Somalia, and Syria), while four Islamic extremist groups (ISIS, Boko Haram, the Taliban, and al Qaeda) were responsible for 74% of all deaths from terrorism in 2015. These groups all have Salafi (Based on looking back to the early years of the religion to understand how contemporary Muslims should practice their faith.[8] They reject religious innovation or *bidah* and support the implementation of *Sharia* (Islamic law) or other Sunni beliefs, (they do not believe that the leader of the faith must be a blood relative of Muhammad and this has caused some conflict, especially with the Shia's, who believe that the line of leadership passes down from Muhammad to his cousin, who was also his son-in-law, Imam Ali ibn Abi Talib and continues down through the family line). The annual number of fatalities from terrorist attacks grew sharply from 2011 to 2014 when it reached a peak of over 32,000, before declining to less than 14,000 in 2019. Many believed this was from the Global Effect of The United States Policies from the President Donald Trumps term in Office.

Since approximately 2000, these terrorist incidents have occurred on a global scale, affecting not only Muslim-majority countries in Africa and Asia, but also Russia, Australia, Canada, Israel, India, the United States, and countries within Europe. Such attacks have targeted both Muslims and non-Muslims, with one study finding 80% of terrorist victims to be Muslims. In a number of the worst-affected Muslim-majority regions, these terrorists have been met by armed, independent resistance groups, state actors and their proxies, and elsewhere by condemnation by prominent Islamic figures.

Some Justifications given for attacks on civilians by Islamic extremist groups come from extreme interpretations of The Quran, the *hadith*, and "*sharia* law". These include retribution by armed *jihad* for the perceived injustices of unbelievers against Muslims. The belief that the killing of many self-proclaimed Muslims is required because they have violated Islamic law and are disbelievers *(takfir)*; the overriding necessity of restoring and purifying Islam by establishing sharia law, especially by restoring the Caliphate as a pan-Islamic state (especially ISIS); the glory and heavenly rewards of martyrdom; the supremacy of Islam over all other religions.

The use of the phrase "Islamic terrorism" is disputed. In Western political speech, it has variously been called "counter-productive", "highly politicized, intellectually contestable" and "damaging to community relations", by those who disapprove of the characterization 'Islamic'. Others have condemned the avoidance of the term as an act of "self-deception", "full-blown censorship" and "intellectual dishonesty".

Daniel Benjamin and Steven Simon, in their book, *The Age of Sacred Terror*, argue that Islamic terrorist attacks are motivated by religious fervor. They are seen as "a sacrament ... intended to restore to the universe a moral order that had been corrupted by the enemies of Islam."

Their attacks are neither political nor strategic but an "act of redemption" meant to "humiliate and slaughter those who defied the hegemony of God".

As an ezample, one of the Kouachi brothers responsible for the *Charlie Hebdo* shooting (A terrorist attack in France in January 2015, claiming the lives of 17 people, including 11 journalists and security personnel at the Paris offices of *Charlie Hebdo*, a satiric magazine), called a French journalist, saying, "We are the defenders of Prophet Mohammed."

According to Indonesian Islamic leader Yahya Cholil Staquf in a 2017 *Time* interview, within the classical Islamic tradition the relationship between Muslims and non-Muslims is assumed to be one of segregation and enmity. In his view extremism and terrorism are linked with "the basic assumptions of Islamic orthodoxy" and that radical Islamic movements are nothing new. He also added that Western politicians should stop pretending that extremism is not linked to Islam.

According to journalist Graeme Wood "much of what" one former major Islamic terror group -- ISIS -- "does looks nonsensical except in light of a sincere, carefully considered commitment to returning civilization to a seventh-century legal environment" of Muhammad and his companions, "and ultimately to bringing about the apocalypse" and Judgement day. ISIS group members insist "they will not—cannot—waver from governing precepts that were embedded in Islam by the Prophet Muhammad and his earliest followers".

Shmuel Bar argues that while the importance of political and socioeconomic factors in Islamist terrorism is not in doubt, "In order to comprehend the motivation for these acts and to draw up an effective strategy for a war against terrorism, it is necessary to understand the religious-ideological factors — which are deeply embedded in Islam."

However, David Shariatmadari (Writer and Editor at the GUARDIAN), asserts the history of Islam argues against Islam being the cause of Islamic terrorism on the grounds that if Islam was the history of jihadi terrorism should go back to the seventh century CE. Instead it is a late 20th and early 21st-century phenomenon, implying (according to Shariatmadari) that the cause of Islamic terrorism is more political than religious.

David Scharia, a counterterrorism official of the United Nations Security Council believes religiously-motivated terrorism (like Islamic terrorism) works by creating an extremist ideological milieu which "legitimizes violence in the name of that ideology". This motivates not only those who are trained, funded, and/or coordinated by terror groups, but also so-called "lone wolf" attackers.

Examining Europe, two studies of the background of Muslim terrorists one of the UK and one of France found little connection between terrorist acts performed in the name of Islam and the religious piety of the operatives. A "restricted" 2008 UK report of hundreds of case studies by the domestic counter-intelligence agency MI5 found that there was no "typical profile" of a terrorist, and that far from being religious zealots, a large number of those involved in terrorism do not practice their faith regularly. Many lack religious literacy and could actually be regarded as religious novices. Very few have been brought up in strongly religious households, and there is a higher than average proportion of converts. Some are involved in drug-taking, drinking alcohol and visiting prostitutes. MI5 says there is evidence that a well-established religious identity actually protects against violent radicalization.

A 2015 "general portrait" of "the conditions and circumstances" under which people living in France become "Islamic radicals" (terrorists or would-be terrorists) by Olivier Roy (French Political Sicentist), found radicalization was not an "uprising of a Muslim community that is victim to poverty and racism: only young people join, including converts".

Roy believes terrorism/radicalism is "expressed in religious terms" because

1. most of the radicals have a Muslim background, which makes them open to a process of re-Islamisation ("almost none of them having been pious before entering the process of radicalisation"), and
2. jihad is "the only cause on the global market". If you kill in silence, it will be reported by the local newspaper; "if you kill yelling 'Allahu Akbar', you are sure to make the national headlines". Other extreme

causes ultra-left or radical ecology are "too
bourgeois and intellectual" for the radicals.

Somewhat in contradiction to this, a study surveying
Muslims in Europe to examine how much Islamist ideology
increases support for terrorism, found that "in Western
countries affected by homegrown terrorism ... justifying
terrorism is strongly associated with an increase in
religious practice". (This is not the case in European
"countries where Muslims are predominant"
Bosnia, Albania, etc. -- where the opposite seems to be
true, i.e. the more importance respondents assigned to
religion in their life, the less likely they were to "justifying
political violence".

Most strains of:
thought/schools/sects/movements/denominations/traditio
ns of Islam do not support or otherwise associate
themselves with terrorism. According to Mir Faizal
(Professor is Physics and Astronomy), only three sects or
movements of Islam the Sunni sects of Salafi, Deobandi,
and Barelvi. have been associated with violence against
civilians. Of the three, only Salafi Islam specifically Salafi
jihadism Islam can be called involved in global terrorism,

as it is connected with Al-Qaeda, ISIS, Boko Haram and other groups. (Terrorism among some members of the Barelvi sect is limited to attacks on alleged blasphemers in Pakistan, and the terrorism among Deobandi groups has "almost no" influence beyond Afghanistan, Pakistan and India.) Another sect/movement known as Wahhabism (intertwined with *non-jihadist Salafism*) has been accused of being the ideology behind Islamic terrorist groups, but Al Qaeda and other terrorists are more commonly described as following a *fusion* of Qutbism and Wahhabism.

Outside of these sects or religious movements, the religious ideology of Qutbism has influenced Islamic terrorism, along with religious themes and trends including Takfir, suicide attacks, and the belief that Jews and Christians are not People of the Book but infidels/kafir waging "war on Islam". These ideas are often related and overlapping.

Qutbism Qutbism is named after Egyptian Islamist theoretician Sayyid Qutb, who wrote a manifesto (known as *Milestones*), while in prison. Qutb is said to have laid out the ideological foundation of Salafi jihadism (according to Bruce Livesey)(an award-winning journalist and investigative reporter); his ideas are said to have formed "the modern Islamist movement" (according to Gilles Kepel)(one of Europe's leading experts on Islamism, the Middle East, and North Africa); which along with other "violent Islamic thought", became the ideology known as "Qutbism that is the "center of gravity" of al-Qaeda and related groups (according to U.S. Army Colonel Dale C. Eikmeier). "Qutb is thought to be a major influence on Al-Qaeda #2 leader, Ayman al-Zawahiri".

In his manifesto (called "one of the most influential works in Arabic of the last half century"), Qutb preached:

- the absolute necessity of enforcement of sharia law ("even more necessary than the establishment of the Islamic belief", without which Islam does not exist)
- the need for violent jihad as well as preaching to bring back sharia law and spread Islam, (a vanguard "movement" will use "physical power and Jihad", to remove "material obstacles")
- that offensive jihad attacking non-Muslim territory should not be neglected by true

Muslims in favor of defensive jihad, (this "diminish(s) the greatness of the Islamic way of life", and is the work of those who have been "defeated by the attacks of the treacherous Orientalists!" Muslims should not let lack of non-Muslim aggression stop them from waging Jihad to spread sharia law because "truth and falsehood cannot coexist on earth" in peace.

- a loathing of "the West" (a "rubbish heap of filth; hollow and worthless")
- which is deliberately undermining Islam (pursuing a "well thought out scheme" to "demolish the structure of Muslim society")
- despite the fact it "knows" it is inferior to Islam (It "knows that it does not possess anything which will satisfy its own conscience and justify its existence", so that when confronted with the "logic, beauty, humanity and happiness" of Islam, "the American people blush")
- and a loathing and hatred of Jews ("world Jewry, whose purpose is to eliminate the limitations imposed by faith and religion, so that Jews may penetrate into body politics of

34

the whole world and then may be free to perpetuate their evil designs such as usury, the aim of which is that all the wealth of mankind end up in the hands of Jewish financial institutions").

Eikmeier(Retired Colonel US Army and Professor at the US Army Command and General Staff college) summarizes the tenets of Qutbism as being:

- A belief that Muslims have deviated from true Islam and must return to "pure Islam" as originally practiced during the time of Muhammad.
- The path to that "pure Islam" is only through a literal and strict interpretation of the Quran and Hadith, along with implementation of Muhammad's commands.
- Muslims should interpret the original sources individually without being bound to follow the interpretations of Islamic scholars.
- Any interpretation of the Quran from a historical, contextual perspective is a corruption, and that the majority of Islamic

35

history and the classical jurisprudential
tradition is mere sophistry.

While Sayyid Qutb preached that all of the Muslim world
had become apostate or jahiliyah (Which is
an Islamic concept referring to the period of time and
state of affairs in Arabia before the advent of Islam in 610
CE), he did not specifically takfir or call for the execution of
any apostates, even those governing non-sharia
governments Qutb did however emphasize that "the
organizations and authorities" of the putatively (refers to
something commonly accepted as true or thought by most
to be true) Muslim countries were irredeemably corrupt
and evil and would have to be abolished by "physical
power and Jihad", by a "vanguard" movement of true
Muslims.

One who did argue this was Muhammad abd-al-
Salam Faraj, the main theoretician of the Islamist
group that assassinated Egyptian President Anwar Sadat.
In his book "Al-Farida al-gha'iba" (The Neglected Duty), he
cited a fatwa issued in 1303 CE by the celebrated strict
medieval jurist Ibn Taymiyyah. He had ruled that fighting
and killing of the Mongol invaders who were invading Syria

was not only permitted but obligatory according to Sharia. This was because the Mongols did not follow sharia law, and so even though they had converted to Islam (Ibn Taymiyyah argued) they were not really Muslims. Faraj preached that rulers such as Anwar Sadat were "rebels against the Laws of God (the shari'ah)", and "apostates from Islam" who have preserved nothing of Islam except its name.

Another Islamic movement accused of involvement in terrorism is known as Wahabism. Sponsored by oil exporting power Saudi Arabia, Wahabism is deeply conservative and anti-revolutionary (its founder taught that Muslims are obliged to give unquestioned allegiance to their ruler, however imperfect, so long as he leads the community according to the laws of God), Nonetheless, this ideology and its sponsors have been accused of assisting terrorism both by:

- Indirectly by "creating" an environment from late 1970s to 2010 that "supported the spread of extremist ideologies"; despite its conservatism, Wahhabism shares important doctrinal points with forms of Islamism a strong "revulsion" against Western influences, a belief in strict implementation of injunctions and prohibitions of sharia law, an opposition to both Shia Islam and popular Islamic religious practices (the veneration of Muslim saints), and a belief in the importance of armed jihad.

- and directly through inadvertent and intentional funding of terrorist groups and through its influence on at least two major terrorist groups the Taliban[and the Islamic State.

Up until at least 2017 or so (when Saudi Crown Prince Muhammad bin Salman declared Saudi Arabia was returning to "moderate Islam"), Saudi Arabia spent many billions, not only through the Saudi government but through Islamic organizations, religious charities, and private sources, on *dawah wahhabiya*, i.e. spreading the Wahhabi interpretation of Islam, This funding incentivized Muslim "schools, book publishers, magazines, newspapers, or even governments" around the world to "shape their behavior, speech, and thought in such a way as to incur and benefit from Saudi largesse," and so propagate Wahhabi doctrines.

The hundreds of Islamic colleges and Islamic centers, over a thousand mosques and schools for Muslim children it financed, often featured Wahhabi-friendly curriculum and religious materials such as textbooks explaining that all forms of Islam except Wahhabism were deviation, or the twelfth grade Saudi text that "instructs students that it is a religious obligation to do 'battle' against infidels in order to spread the faith".

Wahhabi-friendly works distributed for free "financed by petroleum royalties" included those of Ibn Taymiyyah (author of the fatwa mentioned above against rulers who do not rule by sharia law).

Not least, the successful 1980-1990 jihad against Soviet occupation of Afghanistan that inspired non-Afghan jihad veterans to continue jihad in their own country or other benefited from billions of dollars in Saudi financing, as well as "weaponry and intelligence".

The "root cause" of Muslim terrorism is extremist ideology, according to Pakistani theologian Javed Ahmad Ghamidi, specifically the teachings that:

- "Only Muslims have the right to rule, non-Muslims are meant to be subjugated";
- "Modern nation states are unIslamic and constitute kufr (disbelief)";
- the only truly Islamic form of state is a unified Muslim Caliphate;
- "when Muslims obtain power they will overthrow non-Muslim governments and rule";
- "The punishment of kufr (disbelief) and irtidad (apostasy) is death and must be implemented".

Other authors have noted other elements of extremist Islamic ideology.The afterlife and religious justification for killing noncombatants. Al Qaeda justification for the killing of civilian bystanders following its first attack (see above) based on a Ibn Taymiyyah's fatwa was described by author Lawrence Wright, Ibn Taymiyyah had issued a historic fatwa: Anyone who aided the Mongols, who bought goods from them or sold to them or was merely standing near them, might be killed as well. If he is a good Muslim, he will go to Paradise; if he is bad, he will go to hell, and good riddance. Thus the dead tourist and the hotel worker killed by Al-Qaeda would find their proper reward.

An influential tract *Management of Savagery* (*Idarat at-Tawahhush*), explains away mass killing in part by the fact that even "if the whole umma (community of Muslims) perishes they would all be martyrs". Similarly, author Ali A. Rizvi has described the chat room reaction of a Taliban supporter to his (Rizvi's) condemnation of the 2014 Peshawar school massacre that the 132 school children the Taliban slaughtered were "not dead" because they had been killed "in the way of God, "Don't call them dead". They are alive, but we don't perceive it" (citing, Quran 3:169. "And never think of those who have been killed in the cause of Allah as dead. Rather, they are alive with their Lord, receiving provision"), and maintaining that those whose Islamic faith is "pure" would not be upset with the Taliban's murder of children either. (This is truly an Exstremeism of ones self "warped" depiction in Death and purity in the murder of children in the name of Religion).

Superiority of the afterlife

Observers (such as Ibn Warraq) have noted how widely Islamic scripture has emphasized the worthlessness of the temporal world (*Dunya*) in comparison to the hereafter

(*Akhirah*) (example: "O Allah! There is no life worth living except the life of the Hereafter "), and God's anger towards those who do not agree (example: "These are the ones who trade the Hereafter for the life of this world. So their punishment will not be reduced, nor will they be helped" Q.2:86).

Ibn Warraq finds these scripture "remarkably similar" to a number of public statements by **jihadists**:

- "Today you are fighting divine soldiers who love death for Allah like you love life" (Hamas Chief of Staff Muhammad Deif addressing Israelis in 2014),
- "We love death like our enemies love life" (Hamas leader Ismail Haniyeh on Al-Aqsa TV in 2014)
- "The Americans love Pepsi-Cola, we love death." (Afghan jihadist Maulana Inyadullah addressing a British reporter in 2001)
- "The world is but a passage ... what is called life in this world is not life but death" (Ayatollah Khomeini in 1977, commemorating his son's death)

- "...The sons of the land of the two holiest sites (Mecca and Medina) ... I say this to you, These youths love death as you love life" (Osama bin Laden addressing U.S. Secretary of Defense William Perry in 1996 fatwa)

Martyrdom/Istishhad

Terror attacks requiring the death of the attacker are generally referred to as suicide attacks/bombings by the media, but when done by Islamists their perpetrators generally call such an attack *Istishhad* (or in English "martyrdom operation"), and the suicide attacker *shahid* (pl. *shuhada*, literally 'witness' and usually translated as 'martyr'). The idea being that the attacker died in order to testify his faith in God, for example while waging *jihad bis saif* (jihad by the sword). The term "suicide" is never used because Islam has strong strictures against taking one's own life.

According to author Sadakat Kadri, "the very idea that Muslims might blow themselves up for God was unheard of before 1983, and it was not until the early 1990s that anyone anywhere had tried to justify killing innocent Muslims who were not on a battlefield." After 1983 the process was limited among Muslims to Hezbollah (Hezbollah wields significant power in Lebanon, where it operates as both a Shiite political party and militant group) and other Lebanese Shi'a factions for more than a decade.

Since then, the "vocabulary of martyrdom and sacrifice", videotaped pre-confession of faith by attackers have become part of "Islamic cultural consciousness", "instantly recognizable" to Muslims (according to Noah Feldman)(a Harvard Professor and Jounalist), while the tactic has spread through the Muslim world "with astonishing speed and on a surprising course".

First the targets were American soldiers, then mostly Israelis, including women and children. From Lebanon and Israel, the technique of suicide bombing moved to Iraq, where the targets have included mosques and shrines, and the intended victims have mostly been Shiite Iraqis.
In Afghanistan, both the perpetrators and the targets are orthodox Sunni Muslims. Not long ago, a bombing in Lashkar Gah, the capital of Helmand Province, killed

Muslims, including women, who were applying to go on pilgrimage to Mecca. Overall, the trend is definitively in the direction of Muslim-on-Muslim violence. By a conservative accounting, more than three times as many Iraqis have been killed by suicide bombings in just three year (2003–6) as have Israelis in ten (from 1996–2006). Suicide bombing has become the archetype of Muslim violence – not just to Westerners but also to Muslims themselves.

"War against Islam"

A tenant of Qutbism and other militant Islamists is that Western policies and society are not just un-Islamic or exploitive, but actively anti-Islamic, or as it is sometimes described, waging a "war against Islam". Islamists (such as Qutb) often identify what they see as a historical struggle between Christianity and Islam, dating back as far as the Crusades, among other historical conflicts between practitioners of the two respective religions.

In 2006, Britain's then head of MI5 Eliza Manningham-Buller said of Al-Qaeda that it "has developed an ideology which claims that Islam is under attack, and needs to be defended". "This," she said "is a powerful narrative that weaves together conflicts from across the globe, presenting the West's response to varied and complex issues, from long-standing disputes such as Israel/Palestine and Kashmir to more recent events as evidence of an across-the-board determination to undermine and humiliate Islam worldwide." She said that the video wills of British suicide bombers made it clear that they were motivated by perceived worldwide and long-standing injustices against Muslims; an extreme and minority interpretation of Islam promoted by some preachers and people of influence; their interpretation as anti-Muslim of UK foreign policy, in particular the UK's involvement in Iraq and Afghanistan."

In his call for jihad, Osama bin Laden almost invariably described his enemies as aggressive and his action against them as defensive. Defensive jihad differs from offensive jihad by being "fard al-ayn", or a personal obligation of all Muslims, rather than "fard al-kifaya", a communal obligation, (that is, some Muslims must perform it but it is not required of all). Thus, if Al-Qaeda's portrayal of its jihad as defensive has the advantage of tapping into sympathy for victims of aggression, while putting it at the very highest religious priority for all good Muslims.

Emnity towards non-Muslims

In addition to its alleged aggression, Islamist militants, scholars, and leaders support attacks on Christians and Jews on the theological grounds that they are "infidels", and on Western society on the grounds that its secularism and rampant free expression have led to the proliferation

of pornography, immorality, homosexuality, feminism, etc.

An Islamist (Karam Kuhdi) arrested in Egypt in 1981 for his part in a campaign of robbing and killing Christian goldsmiths, explained his reasoning to police interrogating him. Surprised by his non-mainstream beliefs, Kuhdi told them that he and others did not hold with the conventional Islamic doctrine that Christians were "people of the book" and dhimmi subject to protection, but instead were infidels subject to violent jihad. (Tourists—often non-Muslim—were also a common target of Islamic terrorists in Egypt.) Kuhdi quoted Quranic verses: 'Those who say that God is Jesus, son of Mary, are infidels' and 'combat those of the people of the book who are infidels', explaining the Islamists view that the infidels are "the people of the book, since they have not believed in this book".

According to a doctrine known as *al-wala` wa al-bara`* (literally, "loyalty and disassociation"), Wahhabi founder Abd al-Wahhab argued that it was "imperative for Muslims not to befriend, ally themselves with, or imitate non-Muslims or heretical Muslims", and that this "enmity and hostility of Muslims toward non-Muslims and heretical had to be visible and unequivocal".

This principle has been emphasized by Ayman al-Zawahiri (leader of al-Qaeda since June 2011), Abu Muhammad al-Maqdisi (Jihadi theorist), Hamoud al-Aqla al-Shu'aybi (conservative Sudi scholar who supported the 9/11 attacks), and a number of Salafi preachers, Ahmad Musa Jibril, Abdullah el-Faisal.

After the 2016 Orlando nightclub shooting was described as a "hate crime", (the 49 victims murdered in vengeance for American airstrikes against Daesh were customers of a LGBTQ nightclub), Called The PULSE. The official Daesh magazine Dabiq responded: "A hate crime? Yes. Muslims undoubtedly hate liberalist sodomites, An act of terrorism? Most definitely. Muslims have been commanded to terrorize the disbelieving enemies of Allah." (This is how they justify the Slaugter and Murder of innocent People)

Although bin Laden almost always emphasized the alleged oppression of Muslims by America and Jews when talking about the need for jihad in his messages, in his "Letter to America", he answered the question, "What are we calling you to, and what do we want from you?" with

"We call you to be a people of manners, principles, honour, and purity; to reject the immoral acts of fornication, homosexuality, intoxicants, gambling's, and trading with interest. You separate religion from your policies, You are the nation that permits Usury, which has been forbidden by all the religions. You are a nation that permits the production, trading and usage of intoxicants. You are a nation that permits acts of immorality. You are a nation that permits gambling in its all forms. You use women to serve passengers, visitors, and strangers to increase your profit margins. You then rant that you support the liberation of women".

(Bin Laden's belief and his disregard for human life, when it came to Non-Muslims was engrained by his Terrorist activities which included but were not limited to the brutal murder, torcher, and raping of Non-Muslims, and the Attack on America, with the World Trade Center barbarack terrorist attack).

According to traditional Islamic law, the blood of someone who leaves Islam is "forfeit"—i.e. they are condemned to death. This applies not only to self-proclaimed ex-Muslims, but to those who still believe themselves to be Muslims but who (in the eyes of their accusers) have deviated too far from orthodoxy.

Many contemporary liberal/modernist/reformist Muslims believe killing appostates to be in violation of the Quranic injunction 'There is no compulsion in religion. (Q.2:256), but even earlier generations of Islamic scholars warned against making such accusations (known as *takfir*), without great care and usually reserved the punishment of death for "extreme, persistent and aggressive" proponents of religious innovation (*bid'ah*). The danger, according to some (such as Gilles Kepel), was that "used wrongly or unstrainedly, Muslims might resort to mutually excommunicating one another and thus propel the Ummah (The Community) to complete disaster."

Gilles Kepel (Professor at the Institute of Political Studies, Paris), noted that some of Qutb's early followers believed that his declaration that the Muslim world has reverted to pre-Islamic ignorance (Jahiliyyah), should be taken literally and everyone outside of their movement takfired (if u believe there are two Gods, you are considered TAKFIRED); and Wahhabis has been known for their willingness to takfir (A Muslim who declares another Muslim to be an unbeliever or apostate is a *takfiri)* non-Wahhabi Muslims.

Since the last half of the 20th century, a "central ideology" of insurgent Wahhabist/Salafi jihadist groups has been the "sanctioning" of "violence against leaders" of Muslim majority states who do not enforce sharia (Islamic law) or are otherwise "deemed insufficiently religious". Some insurgent groups, Al-Gama'a al-Islamiyya of Egypt, and later GIA, the Taliban, and ISIL), are thought to have gone even further, applying takfir and its capital punishment against not only to Sunni government authorities and Shia Muslims, but to ordinary Sunni civilians who disagree with/disobeyed insurgent policies such as reinstituting slavery.

In 1977, the group *Jama'at al-Muslimin* (known to the public as *Takfir wal-Hijra*), kidnapped and later killed an Islamic scholar and former Egyptian government minister Muhammad al-Dhahabi. The founder of *Jama'at al-Muslimin*, Shukri Mustaf had been imprisoned with Sayyid Qutb, and had become one of Qutb's "most radical" disciples. He believed that not only was the Egyptian government apostate, but so was "Egyptian society as a whole" because it was "not fighting the Egyptian government and had thus accepted rule by non-Muslims". While police broke up the group, it reorganized with thousands of members, some of whom went on to help assassinate the Egyptian president Anwar Sadat, and join the Algerian Civil War and Al-Qaeda. During the 1990s, a violent Islamic insurgency in Egypt, primarily perpetrated by Al-Gama'a al-Islamiyya, targeted not only police and government officials but also civilians, killing or wounding 1106 persons in one particularly bloody year (1993).

In the brutal 1991-2002 Algerian Civil War, takfir of the general Algerian public was known to have been declared by the hardline Islamist Armed Islamic Group of Algeria (GIA). The GIA amir, Antar Zouabri claimed credit for two massacres of civilians (Rais and Bentalha massacres), calling the killings an "offering to God" and declaring impious the victims and all Algerians who had not joined its ranks. He declared that "except for those who are with us, all others are apostates and deserving of death," (Tens, and sometimes hundreds, of civilians were killed in each of a series of massacres that started in April 1998. However, how many murders were the doing of GIA and how many of the security forces—who had infiltrated the insurgents and were not known for their probity—is not known.)

In August 1998 the Taliban insurgents slaughtered 8000 mostly Shia Hazara non-combatants in Mazar-i-Sharif, Afghanistan. Comments by Mullah Niazi, the Taliban commander of the attack and newly installed governor, declared in a number of post-slaughter speeches from Mosques in Mazar-i-Sharif: "Hazaras are not Muslim, they are Shi'a. They are kofr (infidels). The Hazaras killed our force here, and now we have to kill Hazaras. You either accept to be Muslims or leave Afghanistan. ...", indicated that along with revenge, and/or ethnic hatred, takfir was a motive for the slaughter.

From its inception in 2013 to 2020, directly or through affiliated groups, Daesh, "has been responsible for 27,947 terrorist deaths", the majority of these have been Muslims, "because it has regarded them as kafir".

One example of Daesh takfir is found in the 13th issue of its magazine *Dabiq*, which dedicated "dozens of pages to attacking and explaining the necessity of killing Shia", who the group refers to by the label *Rafidah*

Quote from the magazine "Dabiq", (the Shia are an apostate sect drowning in worship of the dead, cursing the best companions and wives of the Prophet, spreading doubt on the very basis of the religion (the Quran and the Sunnah), defaming the very honor of the Prophet, and preferring their "twelve" imams to the prophets and even to Allah! Thus, the Rafidah are mushrik "polytheist" apostates who must be killed wherever they are to be found, until no Rafidi walks on the face of earth, even if the jihād claimants despise such)

Daesh not only called for the revival of slavery of non-Muslims (specifically of the Yazidi minority group), but declared takfir on any Muslim who disagreed with their policy.

According to Daesh, Yazidi women and children (are to be) divided according to the Shariah amongst the fighters of the Islamic State who participated in the Sinjar operations(the Sinjar massacre marked the beginning of the genocide of Yazidis by ISIL, the killing and abduction of thousands of Yazidi men, women and children). Enslaving the families of the kuffar and taking their women as concubines is a firmly established aspect of the Shariah that if one were to deny or mock, he would be denying or mocking the verses of the Koran and the narrations of the Prophet, and thereby apostatizing from Islam.

Starting in 2013, "Daesh" began "encouraging takfir of Muslims deemed insufficiently pure in regard of *tawhid* (monotheism)". The Taliban were found "to be "a 'nationalist' movement, all too tolerant" of Shia. In 2015 ISIL "pronounced Jabhat al Nusrat, then al-Qaida's affiliate in Syria, an apostate group."

Interpretations of the Qur'an and Hadith.

Donald Holbrook, a Research Fellow at the Centre for the Study of Terrorism and Political Violence, analyzes a sample of 30 works by jihadist propagandists for references to Islamic scripture that justifies the objectives of violent jihad. An-Nisa (4:74–75) is quoted most frequently; other popular passages are At-Taubah (9:13–15, 38–39, 111), Al-Baqarah (2:190–191, 216), and Surah (Fight those who do not have faith in Allah nor [believe] in the Last Day, nor forbid what Allah and His Apostle have forbidden, nor practise the true religion 9:5, when these months, prohibited (for fighting), are over, slay the idolaters wheresoever you find them, and take them captive or besiege them, and lie in wait for them at every likely place. But if they repent and fulfill their devotional obligations and pay the zakat, then let them go their way, for God is forgiving and kind.

Holbrook notes that the first part "slay the idolaters" is off quoted but not the limiting factors at the end of the ayat. Peter Bergen (National Security Analyst), notes that bin Laden cited this verse in 1998 when making a formal declaration of war.

Chapter Five

Sharia and Islamic Justice

The Arguing that Muslim blood is more precious than infidel blood, Muslim clerics in and out of Sudan are outraged because a Sudanese court has condemned a Muslim man to death, simply because he murdered American Diplomat John Granville on January 1, 2008.

In a 2009 report that offered certain context: The court had sentenced the men (originally four) to death in June for killing Granville and his driver in January 2008, but the sentence was cancelled in August after (his Muslim driver) Abbas's father forgave the men. Under Islamic law, the victim's family has the right to forgive the murderer, ask for compensation (fedia) or demand execution.Granville's mother, Jane Granville, at the time had asked for the men's execution, but her letter was rejected because it was not "notarized".

The judge said the sentence was confirmed because Granville's family, from Buffalo, in northern New York State, had requested it.

Then, in 2010, the four men convicted of murder, in the words of the U.S. State Department, "escaped from a maximum security prison" in Khartoum. One of the men, Abdul Ra'uf Abu Zaid Muhammad Hamza, was recaptured and is currently in prison awaiting execution.

Finding the punishment unjust, several international Islamic organizations, most recently, the London-based Islamic Media Observatory, have been trying to commute the death sentence, mostly by arguing for Abdul Rauf's "human rights."

However, the Legitimate League of Scholars and Preachers in Sudan (an influential body of Muslim clerics) issued a statement titled "Let no Muslim be killed because of an infidel", a verbatim quote, in fact, from Islam's prophet Muhammad, revealing the true reason why so many Muslims are trying to overturn the death sentence.

The Arabic language statement begins by asserting that "Allah has honored human beings over creation and multiplied the Muslim's honor over the infidel's, because Islam elevates and nothing is elevated above it. The value of the blood of Muslims is equal, or should be, but not so the value of the blood of others." (The Koran itself, e.g., 2:221, confirms this idea that even the lowliest Muslim is superior to any non-Muslim.)

Next, the statement quotes the clear words of Islam's prophet, Muhammad, as recorded in a canonical hadith (form of the Quran as recited and written in which it is religiously binding for the Muslim community): "Let no Muslim be killed because of an infidel." It then elaborates on the meaning of this statement by quoting from "the consensus of Islamic scholars," or *ijma'*, a legitimate source of Islamic jurisprudence.

The Legitimate League of Scholars and Preachers then elaborate on the prophet's injunction as meaning that under no circumstances are Muslim rulers ever permitted to execute Muslims, even if Muslims murder non-Muslims in cold blood, including those groups that are "protected" by Islamic law, such as *dhimmis* (subjugated, tribute-paying non-Muslims) and foreign non-Muslims granted *aman*, or a pledge of security to enter Muslim lands.

Finally, after chastising the offending judge of North Khartoum's felony court, Sayed Ahmed al-Badri, the statement concludes by warning all Muslim rulers and judges "to fear Allah, to apply Allah's law in every matter, whether big or small, to seek justice according to the consensus of Islamic scholars, not to seek to please the infidels, not to rush the verdict, and to know that *Allah prefers the annihilation of the entire earth over the spilling of the blood of one innocent Muslim*".

When American soldiers were accused of desecrating copies of the Koran. The media maelstroms occurred, and grandstanding politicians condemned it. But when the scholars of Islam, quoting the words and teachings of their prophet, openly assert that the "blood of non-Muslims is cheaper than the blood of Muslims", and hence the murder of an American "infidel" by a Muslim cannot be punished blood for blood, this is not even deemed worth reporting by American media or condemned by American politicians.

Chapter Six

The KORAN

THE Koran says the following about the Jews, Christians, and other "unbelievers:"

"O you who believe! do not take the Jews and the Christians for friends; they are friends of each other; and whoever amongst you takes them for a friend, then surely he is one of them; surely Allah does not guide the unjust people." (Sura 5, verse 51).

"And the Jews say: Uzair is the son of Allah; and the Christians say: The Messiah is the son of Allah; these are the words of their mouths; they imitate the saying of those who disbelieved before; may "**Allah DESTROY**" them; how they are turned away" (Sura 9, verse 30).

"And the Jews will not be pleased with you, nor the Christians until you follow their religion. Say: Surely Allah's guidance, that is the "true" guidance, and if you follow their desires after the knowledge that has come to you, you shall have no guardian from Allah, nor any helper." (Sura 2, verse 120).

"And KILL them (the unbelievers) wherever you find them, and drive them out from whence they drove you out, and persecution is severer than slaughter, and do not fight with them at the Sacred Mosque until they fight with you in it, but if they do fight you, then slay them; such is the recompense of the unbelievers." (Sura 2, verse 191).

"Let not the believers take the unbelievers for friends rather than believers; and whoever does this, he shall have nothing of (the guardianship of) Allah, but you should guard yourselves against them, guarding carefully; and Allah makes you cautious of (retribution from) Himself; and to Allah is the eventual coming." (Sura 3, verse 28).

"And guard yourselves against the fire which has been prepared for the unbelievers." (Sura 3, verse 131)

"And when you journey in the earth, there is no blame on you if you shorten the prayer, if you fear that those who disbelieve will cause you distress, surely the unbelievers are your open ENEMY." (Sura 4, verse 101).

"O you who believe! fight those of the unbelievers who are near to you and let them find in you hardness; and know that Allah is with those who guard (against evil)." (Sura 9, verse 123).

"Surely We have prepared for the unbelievers chains and shackles and a burning fire." (Sura 76, verse 4).

"O you who believe! if you obey a party from among those who have been given the Book (The Jews and Christians), they will turn you back as unbelievers after you have believed." (Sura 3, verse 100).

"And their taking usury (interests on money) though indeed they were forbidden it and their devouring the property of people falsely, and We have prepared for the unbelievers from among them a painful chastisement." (Sura 4. verse 161).

"Surely Allah has cursed the unbelievers (Jews, Christians and followers of other faiths) and has prepared for them a burning fire." (Sura 33, verse 64).

"And whoever does not believe in Allah and His Apostle, then surely We have prepared burning fire for the unbelievers." (Sura 48, verse 13).

SO, what does the Koran say about those who turn their back to Islam and commit apostasy?

"They desire that you should disbelieve as they have disbelieved, so that you might be (all) alike; therefore take not from among them (the unbelievers) friends until they flee (their homes) in Allah's way; but if they turn back, then seize them and KILL them wherever you find them, and take not from among them a friend or a helper." (Sura 4, verse 89).

Now, what does the Koran say about women? Here are some quotations:

"Men are superior to women because Allah has made so. Therefore good women are obedient, and (as to) those (women) on whose part you fear desertion, admonish them, and leave them alone in the sleeping-places and BEAT them; then if they obey you, do not seek a way against them; surely Allah is High, Great." (Sura 4, verse 34).

"And as for those who are guilty of an indecency from among your women, call to witnesses against them, four (witnesses) from among you; then if they bear witness confine them to the houses until death takes them away or Allah opens some way for them." (Sura 4, verse 15).

According to the Koran, a woman's testimony is worth half of that of a man.

"O you who believe! when you deal with each other in contracting a debt for a fixed time then call in to witness from among your men two witnesses; but if there are not two men, then one man and two women from among those whom you choose to be witnesses, so that if one of the two errs, the second of the two may remind the other." (Sura 2, verse 282).

As far as sex is concerned, women are sex objects, according to the Koran. They must be ready for intercourse any time the husband wishes so.

"Your wives are a tilth for you, so go into your tilth when you like, and do good beforehand for yourselves, and be careful (of your duty) to Allah, and know that you will meet Him, and give good news to the believers." (Sura 2, verse 223).

During menstruation, however, men should keep away from women; they are filthy. The Koran says:

"It (menstruation) is a discomfort; therefore keep aloof from the women during the menstrual discharge and do not go near them until they have become clean; then when they have cleansed themselves, go in to them as Allah has commanded you; surely Allah loves those who turn much (to Him), and He loves those who purify themselves." (Sura 2, verse 222).

After a Muslim has washed and prepared himself for prayer, he should not touch a woman. Therefore, "pious" Muslims never shake hands with women.

"O you who believe! do not go near prayer until you have washed yourselves; and if you have touched women, and you cannot find water, betake yourselves to pure earth, then wipe your faces and your hands; surely Allah is Pardoning, Forgiving." (Sura 4, verse 43).

In case of inheritance, a woman inherits half of the portion a man inherits:

"They ask you for a decision of the law. Say: Allah gives you a decision concerning the person who has neither parents nor offspring; if a man dies (and) he has no son and he has a sister, she shall have half of what he leaves, and he shall be her heir she has no son; but if there be two (sisters), they shall have two-thirds of what he leaves; and if there are brethren, men and women, then the male shall have the like of the portion of two females; Allah makes clear to you, lest you err; and Allah knows all things." (Sura 4, verse 176).

And what kind of punishment does a thief get, according to the Koran, regardless of how much they steal?

"And (as for) the man who steals and the woman who steals, cut off their hands as a punishment for what they have earned, an exemplary punishment from Allah; and Allah is Mighty, Wise." (Sura 5, verse 38).

Saudi Arabia is one of the the only countries in the world that uses the Koran as its day-to-day law for all kinds of disputes and crimes. It is the Sharia (Islamic law). For Islamists and conservative Muslims, Sharia is the constitution and law that must prevail everywhere. They argue, what is better than the law of Allah which He, via the Engle Gabriel revealed to the Prophet Mohammed 1,400 years ago?

King Abdullah, the absolute monarch of Saudi Arabia, said on a televised speech August 27, 2008, "We do not need democracy, we do not need political parties, we do not need Western human rights, we do not need their freedom of speech. What we need is the Koran. It regulates our life perfectly. It is the best legislation in the history of mankind, it is the word of Allah. There is nothing better than Allah's law."

The "Hadeeth," a collection of statements and comments which Prophet Mohammed allegedly made during his lifetime, is also full of atrocities. Here is a sample:

"A woman came to the Prophet and admitted that she had committed adultery and thereafter became pregnant. The Prophet summoned her husband and all people of Median (in Saudi Arabia). He said, 'This woman committed adultery. Therefore, after she delivers her innocent baby, all of you are going to stone her to death. This is Allah's verdict.' After she delivered her baby she was stoned to death in the center of the town." (Narrated by Muslim, (a close contemporary follower of Mohammed), cited by Khoury, "The Koran", p. 550).

Stoning women and flogging men for adultery are widely practiced in Saudi Arabia and Iran.

The Koran is filled with contradictions. While in sura 2, verse 256, it says "There is no compulsion in religion," it urges Muslims to kill those Muslims who convert to other religions.

Chapter Seven

ISLAM and the INFEDEL

ISLAM Is a mind-control and information-control cult founded by a murderer, torturer, rapist and pedophile called "Mohammed". The mind-control and information-control aspects require that all criticism be silenced.

Has no foundations other than "Mohammed's" murderous rantings (Koran and Hadith). The Koran consists of two conflicting parts, the "Meccan and Medinan" (peaceful and violent respectively). The Medinan stuff supersedes ('abrogates') the Meccan stuff. Muslims act Medinan, but quote Meccan verses to the gullible infidels.

ISLAM claims to worship the same God as Christians and Jews, but in fact worships Allah, a demonic channelling through Mohammed's psychopathic ego. The Death Cult mixes garbled versions of Christian and Jewish scriptures with pagan practices such as moon and meteorite-worship, and cut-throat blood sacrifice of animals and non-believers.

Islam has no real rational, neither philosophical nor theological basis, and the whole belief-system is contradicted by science, philosophy,commonsense, human decency and internal inconsistency.

ISLAM as a whole Cannot withstand rational criticism. It can only spread and maintain itself by ignorance, illiteracy, war, terrorism, and intimidation. Islam has bloody borders and cannot co-exist peacefully with other belief systems. Winston Churchill once said, that, "Islam in a man is as dangerous as hydrophobia (rabies) in a dog".

ISLAM also has a superstitious dread of images of pigs, crosses, Buddhas, Saint George (and his flag). The Islamic women is looked at as semihuman. Wife-beating, incest and child abuse (including mufa'khathat or 'thighing' – the ritual abuse of infants) are encouraged.

ISLAM and all unbelievers (Kaffirs, Kuffar, Kufrs, Kafirs) as ritually unclean subhumans to be killed, subjugated, enslaved, exploited or parasitised. Kafirs are described by the Arabic word 'najis', literally 'filth'. That's why Muslim hatred of Kafirs is intrinsic to their 'religion'. A Kafir doesn't need to do anything to offend a Muslim, his very existence is enough of an affront.

ISLAM's ethical system applies **only** to Muslims. Allah encourages rape, pillage, extortion and enslavement of non-Muslims. Morality does not extend beyond the global gang (ummah). Muslim ethics are somewhat slanted in one direction.

"Allah's" followers are motivated by hatred, greed and lust. There is no love, mercy or compassion. Allah is vindictive, unpredictable, capricious and devious, "Allah leads astray whom he pleases".

ISLAM is the only religion NOT founded on The Golden Rule (the ethics of reciprocity, is an Islamic moral principle which calls upon people to treat others the way they would like). Morality is based on Mohammed's example. If Mohammed did it then it's OK for all Muslims. Hence the encouragement of rape, pillage, subjugation and murder of non-believers and the institutionalised pedophilia prevalent throughout Muslim society (justified by Mohammed's activities).

ISLAM reflects tha all human relations are defined by Dominance/Subjugation. Muslims have schizoid (personality disorder is an uncommon condition in which people avoid social activities and consistently shy away from interaction), and have inferiority/superiority complexes. (A well-balanced Muslim is one with a chip on each shoulder). They respect strength but despise compromise as weakness. Appeasement in its view invites more aggression. The only political system which has been strong enough to subjugate Islam is Stalinism.

ISLAM's practice of Polygamy ensures alpha males get extra women, leading to a shortage of women for the betas. Beta males must either pleasure themselves which is "a sin leading to hell", or form dog-packs and rape or capture kafir women as booty in a razzia (raid for plunder or slaves), or else self-destruct in the presence of infidels, then they can have sex with **72 mythical virgins** in Allah's bordello in the sky. Beta-males are often encouraged by their relatives to become suicide bombers because of the belief that such murderous 'martyrs' will be able to intercede with Allah to take 70 of their relatives to paradise with them.

ISLAM promoting the lying and deception of infidels (taqiyya) is encouraged. This may take many forms, including outright lies, feigned moderation, and condemnation of terrorist attacks to the Kafir while rejoicing with fellow Muslims. All Muslims need to regard themselves as victims of some group of Kafirs so they can harbor grudges against them and against Kafirs in general. Individuals may appear law-abiding and reasonable, but they are part of a totalitarian movement, and must be considered potential killers who can flip in an instant (SJS - 'Sudden Jihad Syndrome').

ISLAM focus shows that Muslims are forbidden to befriend Kafirs except for purposes of **deceit or where conversion may be possible**.

The Koran is Allah's final word and cannot be changed or challenged. To do so is punishable by death. Consequently, Mohammeds Death Cult can never change or be reformed. The instructions to murder and rape infidels are just as valid now as the day they were written. Since Islam cannot be modernized, the Muslims are attempting to Islamise modernity (Muslims involved in the process of reform and renewal, Muslims committed to democracy, or even Muslims intent on reviving the original spirit of Islam). This requires spreading Islam in the West and simultaneously preventing any criticism of the cult by intimidation and PC legislation to curtail freedom of expression.

The Koran, facilitates that Treaties and agreements with Kafirs are made to be broken (Hudna). The word of a Muslim to a Kafir counts for nothing in the eyes of Allah. Allah is The Father Of Lies.

In the Koran, the world is divided between Dar-al-Islam and Dar-al-Harb (the domain of war, the Kufr lands). Muslims living in Dar-al-Harb must work to disrupt their host nations until these can be brought into Dar-al-Islam.

This promotes, that Muslims have **no obligation** to their host nations and in fact are encouraged to parasitise them. Welfare fraud, identity theft, forgery, etc. are endemic in Western Muslim populations, and serious crime against Kafirs (INFIDELS) is regarded as normal and justified. Extortion rackets against Kafirs are mandated by the Koran ('jizya' is the Arabic term for 'protection money' payable by Jews and Christians to the Muslims).

Radicalized Islamists purpotrate that the attack on the host nation isn't just against its religion and economy, but is aimed at its very cultural identity. Islam is a complete system, including a culture, which Muslims regard as superior (despite all evidence to the contrary) to other cultures. Muslims are therefore required to destroy the symbols of 'Jahiliya' (sometimes sp. Jahiliyya) , non-Muslims culture. In the East this has included destruction of Hindu temples and Christian churches and replacement with mosques, and destruction of Buddhist artwork and universities and replacement with heaps of rubble. This process of cultural replacement is now beginning in the West.

Chapter Eight

INFEDEL WOMEN

Much of this traces back to Islamic law. Inherently harsh, its ultimate source is a seventh century Arab man, Muhammad, Sharia is still harsher for women. Men have "authority" over women and may beat them for disobedience. The prophet said women are significantly less intelligent than men, two women are needed to equal one man's testimony, and the majority of hell's denizens consist of women, whom Muhammad further likened to donkeys and dogs in their ability to distract a man from his prayer and thereby annul it.

Such misogyny is confirmed by the headline of a report: (Breibert London) "UK Govt Review into Sharia Admits Systemic Discrimination Against Women. Forced Marriage Victim Made to Appear with Abusers."

If this is Islam's approach to Muslim women, non-Muslim women are doubly damned; not only are they, as infidels, "the enemy" by default, but as females, they are deemed even more inferior than their already despised male counterparts. Add to this the facts that women are physically weaker, and physically more attractive than men, and it becomes clear why they are widely seen as being, at best, "meant for one thing, the pleasure of the Muslim man," as one Muslim told a group of young Christian girls before terrorizing and murdering one. (Koran verses that encourage the sexual enslavement of non-Muslim women and ingrained notions of "sex-on-demand," obviously only propel such thinking.)

The subhuman treatment of non-Muslim women by jihadi organizations such as the Islamic State or Nigeria's Boko Haram, where "infidel" women are bought, sold, gang-raped, mutilated, dismembered and burned alive, is relatively well known (thanks to ISIS itself, for disseminating images and videos). Lesser known is that "infidel" women are treated in similar ways all across the Muslim world.

Unfortunately, more and more women are the target of (Muslim) terrorist groups. There are numerous international incidents of women being kidnapped, raped, and forced to convert from Christianity to Islam by radical extremist groups. Many are also sold on the open market. This brutality is not only occurring in the Middle East but in Africa and in many other places. In many of these countries, women are subject to persecution because they are considered second-class citizens because of their gender. As minorities in both gender and faith, Christian women face double the persecution. Although we don't have an exact number, we know that millions of women are being persecuted, in these Muslim-dominated countries; Christian women are systematically deprived of their freedom to live and are denied basic human necessities.

It is noted that approximately 700 Christian and 300 Hindu girls are abducted, enslaved, and raped in Pakistan every year. These are very large numbers considering that Christians and Hindus each make up only one percent of the nation's Muslim-majority population. After a 9-year-old Christian girl was raped by a Muslim man who boasted of having "done the same service to other young Christian girls," local residents explained: "Such incidents occur frequently.

Christian girls are considered goods to be damaged at leisure. Abusing them is a right. According to the (Muslim) community's mentality it is not even a crime. Muslims regard them as spoils of war." This is why when a young Muslim girl was recently raped and murdered, Pakistan rose up in outrage, whereas the ongoing rape and murder of Christian girls (and boys) is met with deafening silence.

A similar situation prevails in Egypt. Congressman Chris Smith, (New Jersey's 4th District), had testified about the "escalating abduction, coerced conversion and forced marriage of Coptic Christian women and girls. Those women are being terrorized and, consequently, marginalized." Between 2008 and 2013 alone, nearly 600 cases of abduction, rape, and forced conversion of Christian women were documented in Egypt, again, very large numbers considering Christians are roughly only 10 percent of Egypt's population. A former kidnapper recently shed light on how methodical and virtually institutionalized this phenomenon is in Egypt.

Unsurprisingly then, as the number of Muslim migrants continue to grow in Europe, the subhuman treatment and sexual abuse of "infidel" women that was once confined to third world Muslim nations has become a common fixture in the West, and on the same logic. If Christian girls in Pakistan are "meant for one thing, the pleasure of the Muslim man," so a Muslim migrant in Germany who stalked, cursed, and groped a woman told her, "German women are there for sex." She is only one of countless women in Europe to be violated by Muslim men. Even as Western authorities seek to suppress and dissemble over this phenomenon. Even when about 1,000 women were sexually assaulted by Muslim migrants in Cologne, Germany, "the reaction of the Western media, which professes to care about women's rights and well-being, showed censorship and burying the news,"

This is the same reaction most Western media has in the face of migrant crime waves. Witnesses were silenced, or ignored and the media didn't take its responsibility to report the truth seriously. The exact same thing unsurprisingly happened in Sweden, a country that was once a feminist's paradise, where women enjoyed unprecedented liberty and hyper-equality, now known for its sex crimes and gang rapes.

An Article Titled "Rape, Murder and Misogyny: The Real Victims of the Migrant Crisis are Europe's Women," the January 14 Voice of Europe report gives just a few examples:

- In Austria: A 72-year-old grandmother was raped by an Afghan minor; as a result she lost the will to live [and died].
- In Belgium: A young girl was drugged and raped by a migrant after she asked the way to the station.
- In France: Two teens were stabbed to death by a migrant in Marseille.
- In Germany: A 19-year-old student was raped and murdered by an Afghan migrant.
- In Germany: A 17-year-old girl was stabbed to death after quitting her relationship with a migrant.
- In Italy: A Polish woman was gang raped by four migrants in Rimini.

- In the Netherlands: A young girl was raped and almost drowned by an asylum seeker in Kampen.
- In the Netherlands: A woman was gang raped by a group of Africans.
- In Sweden: A girl was stabbed to death after rejecting an asylum seeker.
- In Sweden: A woman in a wheelchair was gang raped by a group of migrants.
- In Switzerland: Six women were sexually assaulted by "dark skinned" men.
- In the UK: Muslim Grooming gangs targeting Takfir girls have been around for decades.

It does bear mentioning that the above examples are only the tip of the iceberg. Among some of the many stories to surface, there were mosque attending Muslims who broke into the home of a British woman and repeatedly raped her at gunpoint; during what was described as a "horrific attack," a Muslim man raped another British woman as she sat on a public bench; three Muslims sexually assaulted a German mother in front of her toddler in the stroller; and pants for women with alarms to ward off rapists sold out almost as soon as they were introduced in Germany.

As the Voice of Europe correctly adds, "Were these acts committed under any other circumstances they would have been classed as either war crimes or crimes against humanity. It is clear, that the real victims of the migrant crisis are Europe's women. They are quickly losing the freedom they fought for and are clear targets for guests who have been accepted into our societies."

To put it differently, all the Hollywood stars, militant feminists and social-justice warriors who are forever raging against "sexism" in the West , but who have nothing to say about Islam's female victims, are not "defenders of women's rights," but pariahs dedicated to subverting Western civilization no less than the terrorists they have been apologizing and essentially covering for.

Chapter Nine

In the development of this book, I wanted to give a broad view of a Culture and Religion; and how it can consume a societies ideologies combining Law and twisted views and writings that propreptuate the killing, Raping and exsterminating all people that do not believe or acknowledge one point of view and beliefs of others.

Western Civilization in general is in direct opposite of ISLAM, ISLAMIC Culture, and SHARIA LAW. Dearborne Michigian, is an example of non-culturlization. What this means is that areas that have been populated with Islamic Fundmentalists and skewed cultural mixing have carved out sections in America as if they transferred themselves from Countries where they fled or alleged to have fled to indoctrine the culture to their own beliefs, and in doing so actually make changes to the indigenous population to mold that society in to what they believe and worship. In reviewing these chapters, you can see that there is conflict here. There are 1.7 Billion Muslims in the world and by 2050 it is estimated to go to possible 2.4 Billion.

In considering the views are extreme with ISLAMIC Terrorism, one can conclude that when one feels that it is there Duty to enforce Religious and Cultural beliefs to the point of Killing innocent Men, Women, and Children, then reassessing how one lets this ideology influence into a society that promotes freedom of Religion, freedom of personal Choice, Freedeom of Sexual Identities and Profrences, freedom of expression, then one needs to restrict that group that would limit these freedoms. The influence of SHARIA Law and Islamic Exstreism is limited to those pockets in Countries that tolerate and promote Islamic Fundementalism and then tolerate and or promote SHARIA LAW. Say one thing and then do another.

***NOT** all Muslims by any means promote the ideology of SHARIA LAW, and the Extreme views that are prolificated by that small minortity that would perverse the interpretation of the KORAN and Force others to strictly follow SHARIA LAW., laws that treat women as second class not equaling a man in any way. Women are not allowed to leave their homes without a male. They cannot Drive a vehicle. They cannot Vote. They cannot go to school. They have no freedom, and it is promoted to beat women when necssasry according to SHARIA. For our LGBTQ Communities under SHARIA LAW you would all be subject to **immediate Death**. Murders are carried out daily in Afghanistan to their LGBTQ Communities.*

BUT, as you can see with what had recently occurred in Afghanistan with the US pulling its troops out, the Country had Fallen before the US left. This occurred on August 30th, 2021, and you can see where there were MUSLIM's, Men, Women and Children hanging off US planes and trying anything they can to leave, so they would not be under the Talliban Rule, and governed by SHARIA LAW. They believe in Freedom, they believe in Democracy, they want ALL their children to be able to be whatever they wish to be in life, to be able to be educated, worship what they wish, to be able to love who they want to love, regardless of race, religion, or sexual preference.   This unfortunately is an ideology that is in direct **opposite** of the ISLAMIC Exstremism and SHARIA LAW that is very real, and is very much here, being embedded in Wester Civilization.

If you really want to see what America will look like in the near future if this goes unchecked and not stopped, take a picture of what "Afghanistan" looks like right now. That could be the future for you, your children and their children.

DEDICATION:

For All the Men, Women and Children of every Religion and Faith, that have lost their lives to murderous cowards that hide behind Religion to justify their barbaric twisted lust for power and dominance over others.

WAKE UP!!!!! IF NOT FOR YOURSELVES, THEN FOR YOUR CHILDREN!!!

أَكُ   الله

Darren W. Freeman